Anna's Room

CW00344347

A Play

Ellen Dryden

Samuel French - London
New York - Sydney - Toronto - Hollywood

ANNA'S ROOM

First produced in the Birmingham Repertory Studio Theatre on 9th February 1984 with the following cast of characters:

Anna 2	Mary Rutherford
Simon Field	Ian Redford
Anna Wentworth (Anna 1)	Petra Markham
Prue Warren	Tessa Peake Jones
Dan Warren	Tristram Wymark
Harriet Warren	Sylvia Kay

Directed by Peter Farago
Designed by Geoffrey Scott

The action takes place in Anna 1's attic room

Time—the present

For Don. With love.

AUTHOR'S NOTE

It is important that the set should consist of the two "walls" of a square room, set diagonally to the audience. There should be a practical door. The window, radiator, fireplace etc. referred to as part of the room can be real—on the existing "walls"—or imagined on the two non-existent "walls" depending on the wishes and the resources of the company.

Ellen Dryden

ACT I*

As the Lights come up we see two sides of a square box set diagonally to the audience. The walls are gauze and there is the suggestion of a sloping attic roof. There is a door UL and a window in the wall R with a radiator underneath. Apart from a telephone in the corner and a tea-chest, the room is quite empty

Music. Remote and detached

After a moment a woman comes on to the stage. She looks at the space in front of her. She is dressed very simply in a plain dark-coloured, rather long dress. We shall come to know her as Anna 2. She has a piece of paper in her hand—the blurb from an estate agent. She has a piece of chalk too and with this she very deliberately draws on the floor the two remaining "walls" of the room. She stands quite still looking in front of her.

The music fades

Anna 2 (*holding the paper in front of her but not reading from it*) with a delightful study/third bedroom. Thirteen feet six by eleven feet ten into bay. Immaculate decor. Fine view over park. Cosy bathroom. Low-level suite. Avocado fittings. Small well-appointed kitchen. Gas cooker. Small fridge. Would suit young couple. Or business people sharing. No children. No pets. NB. No lift. (*Her voice is quite unemphatic. Almost expressionless. She lets her hand holding the paper fall to her side. Slowly*) Would suit—Anna nicely.

She moves out of sight into the shadows away from the room area

Anna 1 and Simon Field come in

Anna 1 is wearing an identical dress to Anna 2. But she also has on a jacket, scarf, odd bits of jewellery, etc. which makes the whole outfit look quite different. Simon is a dark watchful man who would prefer to remain silent but allows confidences to be wrenched out of him at times, then steps back as if dissociating himself from what he has said. Anna 1 is a lively, quick-witted, fairly extrovert person, apparently. But there is a slightly over-emphatic nerviness about her which sometimes surfaces in a too extreme reaction to some quite minor incident

Simon is half-pushing/half-carrying a tubular steel corduroy-covered easy chair, over which is draped a velvet jacket. Anna 1 also has the estate agent's blurb

Simon Where do you want this? And I'm not pushing it down that passageway again.

Anna 1 Oh ... Anywhere here'll do.

---

*NB Paragraph 3 on page ii of this Acting Edition regarding photocopying and video-recording should be carefully read.

He puts the chair down where he stands and sits in it. Anna 1 is looking out of "her" window, consulting the paper. Simon watches her

Well that's true at least. It is a fine view over the park ... I like these old houses. They've always got unexpected bits to them. Like those steps down, in the bathroom ... I suppose these were the servants' quarters ... when the house was built—that tiny fireplace. God! I bet it was cold up here in the winter! (*She laughs*) God bless Alastair J. de Courcey and gas central heating!

Simon is impassive

Isn't it marvellous having a landlord called Alastair J. de Courcey? You should see him too. He's like something out of Henry James. Prue and I didn't dare look at each other when we went to see him in his offices— er chambers, I suppose?—in the Inns of Court. Ha! (*Crossing to the window expansively*) Oh and look at all that air! Now tell me—weren't we right to get out of Central London?

Simon (*drily*) You'll have a long drive to school.

Anna 1 I think I might get a bike. In fact, I'm going to start being terribly healthy. I shall always run up all those stairs. I'll sell the car—I'll only get the price of a bike for it anyway. And I'll quit eating junk food. It rots your body you know. I'll live on nuts and honey and wheatgerm and, and *bran*!

She is watching Simon as she speaks. This over-enthusiastic performance is for his benefit and he is obviously unimpressed.

(*Quietly*) I—thank you for helping me move my stuff.

Simon I'll go and get your case. Where do you want that? In the bedroom?

Anna 1 looks at him

Anna 1 (*quickly*) Bedrooms!

Simon does not answer

Mine is the little one at the back. I'm having this room as my study. So Prue is having the big bedroom.

Simon says nothing

Well, she needs a study as well. But she won't be here as much as me so we thought that that was the best way to arrange things... (*Her voice trails away*)

Simon Very sensible.

Pause. Anna 1 snaps irritably at him

Anna 1 Oh, for God's sake, Simon.

Simon What?

Anna 1 You've been niggling away at this for—for days.

Simon You're imagining things.

Anna 1 No. I'm not! It's you who's imagining things. And you just bloody well won't say them. This wall of silence is just—creepy. If you want to know if I'm (*with heavy irony*) "having an affair" as you'd probably put it, with Prue, you could ask me. But stop being so prurient. It makes me sick.

Simon I don't want to know.

Anna 1 (*sulkily*) Then why won't you talk to me any more?

Simon I've got nothing to say.

Anna 1 Don't be so pompous.

Simon I'll bring your desk in here then. Then I'll push off.

Anna 1 No. Stay and have supper with me—please. Please Simon.

Simon When's Prue getting here?

Anna 1 Not till tomorrow. Please Simon. I don't want to be on my own.

Simon You want jam on it don't you? I've got work to do.

Anna 1 (*wheedling*) Do it here! I've got a pile of essays to mark. I could make coffee and beans on toast or something and we could sit here and work together. It would be like—old times.

Simon looks at her incredulously

Simon (*wearily*) For Christ's sake Anna! You are the most selfish bloody female I have ever met. It's not that you don't admit to other peoples' feelings—it never crosses your mind that they might have any!

Anna 1 Oh well, if you're going to go on sulking for ever. St Simon the Martyr!

Simon (*with a flash of anger*) Look Anna, you told me out of the blue you were moving out of our flat—you didn't even bother to tell me you were looking for this place. Then suddenly it's "Simon, will you give me a hand moving to my new flat. I need a change!" I drag bloody furniture and books over here like a fool—not asking any questions and you casually inform me you're moving in with Prue. I don't even ask if you're chucking me for Prue and you accuse me of being dirty-minded. God knows I'm not exactly trying to trap you—but does it infringe your female integrity just to tell me what's going on?

Anna 1 You just want to—there was to be no ownership—

Simon And I stuck to my side of the bargain. Doesn't that entitle me to any consideration whatsoever?

Anna 1 You sound like my father.

Simon Not all your father's ideas are such bad ones.

Anna 1 *You* could have—*I* didn't try to hang on to *you*.

Simon Yes. I could have walked out on—left—you. But I didn't. There isn't a neutral word for what you've done is there? Terminated our arrangement. Pissed off without a word.

Anna 1 I'm sorry if you're bitter about it. I have a right to live where I want to though, haven't I?

Simon Sure. You will note I haven't said a word to stop you.

Anna 1 Then why are you so—angry about it?

Simon You know perfectly well, Anna.

Anna 1 No I don't.

Simon You are confusing freedom and irresponsibility.

Anna 1 That is the most pompous thing I've ever heard.

Simon Maybe. But the only restraints in our relationship were what you imagined. I asked nothing of you, but we came up against this insuperable barrier. I'm a man. And in your new little world of half-baked ideas and half-digested bits of *The Guardian*'s woman's page that means I'm an aggressive predator. Full stop. Get your persecution mania right Anna. You're like the man with the chronic stutter who said they wouldn't employ him as a radio announcer because he was a Jew.

Anna 1 looks at him appraisingly

Anna 1 I think on balance I prefer people like old Hemsby at school. His favourite saying—brought out on all occasions is—"All motorists should be shot and all women hanged". He always stands up when you come into the room. And the way he holds the door open for you is a studied assertion of supremacy. But I think I prefer that to the "some of my best friends are women" approach. Or you. "I'm so sensitive and understanding I'd have made a better woman than any I've ever met!"

Simon And will Prue get the supper for you when you've got a load of marking and you don't feel like cooking?

Anna 1 I don't know. I haven't asked her. You think you deserve the Order of Merit because you can on rare occasions cook a cheese omelette. Little girls aren't born with their "Homemaker's Badges" stamped on their arms you know.

Simon This is futile. There's no need to get so emotional.

Anna 1 Aaaaaargh!!! Yes. I agree. We have three facts to consider. a) I shared a flat with you. b) I moved out. c) I am going to share a flat with Prue. Subject closed.

Simon Four facts. d) I am still here.

Anna 1 looks quickly at him

I don't cease to exist when you move on.

Anna 1 looks searchingly at him. Music. A nocturne by John Field. The Lights fade to an oval of light in the centre of the stage. Anna 1 crosses behind the chair and stands, her hands resting lightly on the back of the chair. She is in the shadows. We cannot see her face

Anna 2 moves into the chair and sits. She has an embroidery ring and sews tranquilly

Simon slips on the velvet smoking jacket and cravat which were on the chair. He moves into the pool of light and stands looking at Anna 2. She is wearing a fichu and an overskirt over her plain dress. Her dress and Simon's stance and dress suggest a Victorian vignette. The music continues. Pause. Anna 2 looks up and smiles. The music fades as they begin to speak

Anna 2 Mr Field! How kind of you to—Father told me you were to visit him this afternoon—

Simon (*smiling*) Oh, Miss Wentworth, you surely didn't imagine I would go away without seeing you.

Anna 2 (*coyly*) But I know how busy you are. I can't expect to encroach upon your time when ever you come to see Papa.
Simon (*indicating her embroidery*) But you are busy too!
Anna 2 (*wincing*) Don't Laugh at me Mr Field. Embroidering chair covers! (*She pushes aside her frame irritably*)
Simon But you do it so exquisitely.

Anna 2 lowers her head. Then looks at him resolutely

Anna 2 I have begun to read the book you sent me.
Simon Good.
Anna 2 Father has it now. He—my eyes were troubling me—(*With a slight laugh*) He said it was hardly a book for a female. (*She bends her head*)
Simon (*gravely*) I think your father does not always—(*choosing his words carefully*)—truly value your understanding.
Anna 2 (*dully*) He has every concern for my welfare. But I am not his son.
Simon Of course.
Anna 2 (*bitterly as if quoting*) To have three daughters who are born lusty and thrive through infancy, throwing off every childish ailment with ease, and survive into healthy adulthood—and then to lose your only son at birth—together with his mother—is the cruellest blow fate can impose on a man!
Simon (*neutrally*) But Mr Wentworth is an exemplary father.
Anna 2 Oh yes! It's only on winter evenings when the fire is blazing and the curtains are drawn and the rain lashes the windows that he looks at his three daughters—all eagerly ministering to his comfort—and he realizes that—he has no future. And he sighs and speaks tenderly to us and we know that we have failed him. And I am the biggest failure of all.
Simon Anna—
Anna 2 Can you imagine how often he has looked at me and shaken his head and said "Anna, my dear. You have a quick intelligence, a good mind. If only—"

There is a pause

Simon Miss Wentworth, thoughts like this will destroy your peace of mind—and injure your every relationship. You mustn't sit here like this letting these ideas spread like poison through—
Anna 2 The afternoons are very long, Mr Field. Running my father's household takes very little time—and very little thought. The servants are reliable. Mrs Thompson humours me very sweetly when I give her her orders for the day. It's a game we play you see. Pretending that I—
Simon Anna; I have something to ask you. Please don't go on.
Anna 2 Oh?
Simon (*carefully*) If you dislike ordering your father's household—would you—could you take on the ordering of mine?

Anna 2 looks bleakly at him

Your father has given me permission to approach you, to ask you. Will you do me the honour of becoming my wife?

There is a pause

Anna 2 (*flatly*) No. I couldn't possibly.

A pause

Simon Am I so distasteful to you?

Anna 2 No. No it isn't that. I couldn't—it would be—(*Giving up and relying on the accepted formula*) Thank you for the honour you have done me Mr Field, but I cannot escape the confines of my father's house by entering into a marriage—

Simon —which would give you the freedom of your own household and the dignity of a married woman. Anna, you are no longer a girl. Surely you cannot wish to dwindle into an old maid. Dependent on the charity of your relations. You have too much spirit for that.

Anna 2 A piece of property. A parcel handed from one man to another. Then my sister moves into my place until another parcel hunter comes along. Then my youngest sister. Until my father is left with a house-keeper. And the only difference he notices is that he no longer has the expense of three great girls about the house. And the bother of remembering to be fond of them. And we girls move into a stranger's house. We are afforded courtesy and respect as a matter of course. Because that is easier than liking us. And we bear—in pain and incomprehension—more daughters to disappoint our husbands.

Simon (*gently*) These are unwomanly thoughts, Anna. Your reading has embittered you. I am not an unreasonable man. Many a man would consider you—

Anna 1 No. No. No. No. No. No.

The lights come up on the whole stage. Anna 1 shakes her hands vigorously to stop what is happening

Anna 2 slips quietly away

Simon (*present day*) I am not an unreasonable man, Anna.

Anna 1 (*remotely*) No?

There is a loud insistent peal of the doorbell. Pause

Simon Are you expecting anyone?

Anna 1 No.

Simon I'll see who it is.

Simon exits

Anna 1 looks round anxiously. Very faintly a few bars of the Field Nocturne are heard, a little distorted. Anna 1 puts her hand to her head and shakes her head slightly

Anna 1 No. It must stay empty ... I don't want ... intruders. (*She moves to the chair and runs her hand gently over the back of the chair*)

Simon comes in with Prue

Prue is lean, dark-haired, eager-looking. She has a sureness Anna 1 lacks.

But at the moment she is rather off-balance. She is pale and shaken and holding a handkerchief to her head. Anna 1 stares at her stupidly. Simon leads Prue to a chair and sits her down

Prue! I didn't think you were coming till tomorrow.

Prue I wasn't—

Simon (*brusquely to Anna 1*) Never mind that now. Have you got any plasters and—oh I don't know TCP or something—handy. Now! Cotton wool and stuff.

Anna 1 Why? What's happened?

Simon In a minute. Just get the stuff.

Anna goes out

(*To Prue*) are you all right?

Prue Yes. I'm OK. More shaken than hurt actually. (*She moves the hanky from her forehead. It is heavily bloodstained*) Whoops!

Simon Do you need a doctor?

Prue (*giggling weakly*) I *am* a doctor!

Simon No. Come on. That looks a bit—

Prue It's only a graze. You always bleed like a stuck pig from a cut on the head. Is there a mirror anywhere? I don't think I need stitches. (*She shakes her arm ruefully*) My wrist is worse actually.

Anna 1 comes back with a bowl of hot water and a clean white pillow-case

Anna 1 I can't find a thing. It's all just boxes ... We'll have to rip up this pillowcase. Here. Tear some strips. (*She hands it to Simon and rips off a chunk for herself and begins to bathe Prue's head*)

Prue Ow! I see why you went in for teaching. You lack the ministering angel touch and then some!

Anna 1 Oh. It's nothing much.

During the next speeches Anna 1 ties a strip of pillowcase round Prue's head which gives her a distinctly rakish look

I don't know if I've got any antiseptic. Do you think it'll be all right? It seems clean enough. What happened? Did you fall over?

Prue No. I was mugged!

Anna 1 (*amazed*) You what?

Prue Well. Half mugged. As I came out of the station—down that little passageway at the back of the houses—a youth—well a kid—he was about fourteen, I suppose—jumped me ... It was sort of ludicrous. He waved—oh, a cricket stump or rounders bat or something at me and said he was going to bash my brains out ... Presumably he should have been at Games somewhere. I said, "Don't be silly. I haven't got any money. Put that down!" and I held out my hand and pushed the bat or whatever aside ... He dropped the damned thing! And it rolled into the gutter. Then he got hysterical. He swore at me and grabbed hold of me and shook me and shouted. He was—I think he was crying. He was like a toddler having a tantrum. We just sort of scuffled—he was trying to grab my bag. Then he caught me across the face with the back of his hand and—this is the result! He was wearing one of those flash rings ... all this deal of blood is from a very minor scratch! (*Her voice is a little shaky. Against her will. She lowers her head and bites her lip*)

Anna 1 Is it very painful?

Prue No ... My pride took the biggest dent. It is a bit ghastly being mauled around like that. He was much stronger than me as well—which was fairly humiliating. A couple more people came down the passageway and he ran off ... He was pretty half-hearted about the whole affair actually ... (*She holds her head*) I expect I was his first.

Simon He managed to split your head open anyway.

Prue A four-year-old with a well-aimed Tonka toy could do that. Human heads are pretty badly designed from the walloping angle! (*She gets up, slightly shaky and holds out her wrist and twists it, wincing with pain. She looks at it ruefully*) There's nothing broken. Just badly wrenched where he grabbed me. But that's going to be the real trouble ... (*With a sharp intake of breath as she moves her hand*) It's some ludicrous atavistic urge that makes you hang on to your property ... I've got ... a handkerchief ... a doorkey, the *New Statesman* and one pound seventy-eight in that bag. And I wouldn't let go the damn thing. (*She crosses to the tea-chest and looks in the mirror. She laughs*) Oh, well done Anna. I look like something out of a Victorian painting. The wounded drummer boy.

Simon (*to Anna 1*) Have you unpacked any coffee?

Anna 1 Yes. There's a bag of stuff on the draining-board.

Simon I'll make some for us.

He goes out

Prue (*with a grin*) He's still speaking to you then?

Anna 1 Just. You weren't supposed to be here till tomorrow.

Prue No. I know. I just had some spare time and I thought I'd look in. Listen. Can I bring my brother with me tomorrow—for a few days? He's turned up suddenly and he's got nowhere to go. He's very quiet and clean.

Anna 1 Ye—es. I don't mind.

Prue Good. Thanks. Well. I suppose I'd better have this coffee and disappear. It didn't occur to me Simon would be here.

Anna 1 Well, that doesn't matter.

Prue sits and holds her head a little wearily

Prue I've had one bang on the head today. I'm not going to get caught in your cross-fire.

Anna 1 There isn't a battle. I don't like fights.

Prue (*with a little ironic half laugh*) Ha ah ... This (*pointing to her head*) will probably make me a better person. All doctors should be beaten up regularly ... (*Remotely*) I spent a fair bit of the other night, fed up to the back teeth—patching up this bloody irritating woman with a black eye, a broken arm, badly bruised ribs and a four-inch gash across her

cheekbone—She sat there bleeding—just crying quietly. Slipped on the
kitchen floor she had!! No. Nobody had touched her. She'd banged her
cheek on the side of the dresser ... I even descended to the woman to
woman approach—you can tell me. I'd understand. But no. Kitchen
floor. So I left it. Patched her up. They admitted her—she was in such
a bad way ... tucked her up in bed. The sister said we've had her in
here before! Fell down the stairs last time! Broke her jaw ... She dis-
charged herself the next day. Had to get back to the children. Nice
respectable, quiet little woman. Wouldn't even run to a refuge—to others
in the same boat. Wouldn't talk to another woman—if she'd been a kid
I could have gone into action. As it was—I was just glad to see the back
of her.

Simon comes in with a tray of coffee

Simon Coffee. (*He sets the coffee down*)

*Music plays to denote the passing of time. The Lights fade. Prue and Simon
bring on plates and cutlery. When the Lights come up again, they sit com-
panionably in the warm light—Anna 1 on the tea-chest, Prue in the chair,
Simon stretched out on one elbow on the floor. They have just had supper.
They are relaxed and cheerful*

Prue Baked beans on toast with melted cheese on top is actually one of
the great experiences of life.
Simon (*wryly*) You'd better make the most of it. Anna's going macro-
biotic.
Anna 1 Me? Oh yes ...
Prue Why?
Simon (*with a touch of bitterness he can't hide*) Moving out to Ealing and
a flat on the edge of a park is a major break with urban squalor. You're
going to have window boxes full of bean sprouts and alfalfa!
Anna 1 You can sneer as much as you like ...
Simon Oh no. Perish the thought! It can cost a hell of a lot though living
the simple life. You have to find the right little shop with the right gritty
kind of lentils and blackeyed beans. Then you lug them home in recycled
paper bags that split and leave a little trail of brown rice and mouse
droppings all the way home. Just like the babes in the wood.
Anna 1 (*sweetly*) More dandelion coffee?
Prue I'm not going to live on health foods. I had enough of that when I
was a kid. My mother was obsessional about my teeth and my bowels.
They used to laugh at me at school. There was a sweet shop outside my
primary school. And everybody tumbled out at half-past three and
bought Mars bars and iced lollies and crisps and Kola Kubes and rhu-
barb and custard sweets. And I wasn't allowed any of them. And when
I moaned at my mum that everybody had something nice when they
came out of school she brought me a little bag of carrots and raisins
... and nuts. I could have died. There were some girls in the juniors that
saw it and until the day they left they used to put their fingers to their
heads like this—(*she puts her fingers, like donkey's ears to the side of her*

head—and shout "Hee Haw". Poor Mum. (*She sits back*) Of course I haven't got any fillings (*mock-dramatically*) except on my soul! I never said anything to her though. My brother didn't either. He just organized a protection racket in the playground. Threatened all the little kids with instant death if they didn't pay him a percentage of their sweet money. He was brilliant. He never took more than a penny from any one child. But he'd got about eighteen or nineteen victims so he always ended up richer than anybody. Never gave me any ...

Anna 1 (*delicately*) And this is the brother you are bringing here?

Prue Oh well, he's changed a bit since then. (*With a grin*) No he hasn't. He's all right though. Anyway the point is, include me out of the lentils. I like real rubbish food ... I like bacon sandwiches with sliced white bread and brown sauce. Peanut butter with Marmite. Frozen chips. Fish fingers. Spaghetti hoops. Cup cakes. Bright pink blancmanges. Tinned peaches. Jelly that hasn't quite set, swimming with evaporated milk. But my very favourite food of all is corned-beef fritters.

Anna 1 (*laughing*) You're not serious are you?

Prue Oh yes I am! (*Clasping her hands together*) We are what we eat. And that's me.

Simon Sounds like you've been irredeemably corrupted by hospital canteens.

Prue No. I am a child of my time. Have you ever shelled a pound of peas? All that work and all those maggots crawling about and all those nasty little black bits. You finish up with a teaspoonful of rock hard green pellets, and a great pile of maggotty pods. Because all the best ones have gone to Birds Eye, anyway. I don't believe in leaving anything to nature. My only concession to healthy living is prunes every morning to keep me regular ... But I do like them as well.

Simon Not senna pods?

Prue Never actually seen a senna pod. I like those little bits of chocolate though. '

Anna 1 You have the fridge and I have the store cupboard then.

Prue bends her head and holds her brow for a moment

Simon Are you all right?

Prue A bit woozy. It'll pass.

Silence. Broken suddenly by the two-tone blare of a police car or ambulance. It becomes louder then fades away. Then another begins. Anna crosses to the window and looks out

Anna 1 Police. They're in a hurry.

Simon Probably going off duty.

Anna 1 It's a dreadful noise isn't it? Wonder what they're doing up here?

Simon (*irritably*) Oh don't be so childish Anna. You haven't moved to the Garden of Eden. Just because you've got a few trees to look at instead of railway sidings you haven't taken a lease on the Earthly Paradise. They have drunks, derelicts, prostitutes, bankrobbers what have you here too you know.

Prue And muggers!

Anna 1 (*pleadingly*) Yes. Of course. I know that ... it's just ... don't you
find it disturbing? The ordinary day to day things we're supposed to—
live with. I mean, we're all very good at—not ... living with (*she chooses
her words carefully*) the big terrors—the really dreadful things. (*With a
little laugh. Almost in inverted commas*) Northern Ireland. The Bomb
... the Third World War ... You say to yourself oh I can't think about
that. It's dreadful but there's nothing I can do ... Or you get involved
in some organization or pressure group. And that's hiding too in a way
... the rules of the group take over ... Who's the chairman? How do we
get our point across? It's like going to church, every Sunday if you're
religious. You don't think about God and Christ dying on the cross.
You think those flowers are a bit wilted and there are finger-marks on
that brass.

Simon (*dismissively*) Agonizing about the world may be an indulgence but
it's a favourite occupation—and it always has been. We have a few
years—each—to get through ... We choose our own—targets for compassion or anguish.

*Anna 1 looks at him quickly. His face has closed. His thoughts have obviously
turned inward on some awkward thoughts of his own*

Anna 1 But—you have to ignore so much—just take it for granted. That's
life. Like Prue being mugged. We just think, oh these things happen.
Tough. The finger pointed at you. Could have been worse. What do you
expect if you're a woman and you go about on your own?

Prue I shall still use that alleyway—in the erroneous—but human assump-
tion that lightning doesn't strike twice in the same place.

Anna 1 Did the people who came along help you?

Prue No.

Anna 1 (*sadly*) No. They don't ... I was in Leicester Square the other
week. There was an old "down and out" in a shop doorway sitting on
some steps ... He looked like an alcoholic. Very dirty ... ragged. A big
overcoat—although it was a hot night. Mottled sort of face. Red eyes.
He was just rocking to and fro. And there was a girl lying with her head
in his lap. She was very ... young. Pale. Jeans. Check shirt. A bit grubby
but not a—derelict. It was about seven o'clock in the evening. Crowds
everywhere. Going to the cinema. Theatre. Just strolling. Nobody did
anything. People just looked—and said "Mmm. Drugs I suppose. She's
very young." There were two elderly women who were obviously fascin-
ated, they kept looking while they were waiting to cross the road ...
We've seen documentaries on the telly you see. We all know about drug
addicts. So we all just went off to wherever we were going.

Prue (*brutally*) She might just have been tired.

Anna 1 It was very upsetting though. And we just shrug and say "What
can you do?" People go to hell their own way. We all start out so clean
and beautiful—and look at us after a few years. Drunk. Diseased. Obese.
Spoiled. Don't you ever look at—oh—murderers or what have you and
think of them as babies? All soft and lovely.

Prue (*disgusted*) Don't be sentimental, Anna. We don't even start out right. It's an obstacle race and some of us have bigger handicaps than others from day one. It shook me—when I was a student—on the maternity ward. There was an alcoholic mum—with a drunk baby. They didn't even take her gin away from her. Even if they could have found it. She was going to take that baby home. She'd got to cope—drunk or sober. You can't tidy everybody up. It's no use pretending you can. You should try a few nights on casualty. (*She yawns and stretches*)

Anna 1 Yes. When I was very small I told my mother I wanted everything to be "nice and nice". It got to be a family saying ...

Simon (*abruptly*) I'll be off.

Prue You can walk me to the tube. I don't want to meet my peripatetic rounders buff again.

Anna 1 Oh. Are you going?

Prue Yes. I move in tomorrow.

Simon And I have a flat to go to!

Anna 1 I thought you could stay ...

Prue No gear. Anyway I've got things to do. Thanks for supper. See you tomorrow.

She goes out

Simon (*drily*) You can have your little world to yourself for a night. Sweep it clean. Wipe off the finger-marks.

Anna 1 Don't sneer.

Simon No. (*He puts his hand against her cheek. Then leans forward and kisses her forehead lightly*) Good-night.

He goes out

Anna 1 is left standing quite alone in the middle of the room. The Lights change to a cold white. The walls take on a stone-like quality. Music from far away. Plainsong. A shadow is thrown on the floor—the elongated shape of an arched cell window

Anna 2 enters. A fourteenth-century nun. She moves towards the shadow of the window. She is backlit, the light shining round her.

Anna 1 All to myself—myself—myself. (*She moves into the shadows*).

Anna 2 (*her hands lightly clasped*) This then is my portion. Dear Lord, Save me from pride, from vanity and from sloth—I am your votaress —the Bride of Christ ... No! ... The Lady Ann skilled in music, embroidery and the womanly arts—youngest daughter of the House. Consigned to a nunnery because there was no husband for the Lady Ann. Safe. Safe within these walls, Lord. Here with all the other brides of Christ. Married to God because no earthly husband ... no, forgive me Lord ... Let me find peace ... from the world ... the—flesh—and the Devil ... Let me worship you aright ... (*She looks up, afraid*) And dear Lord, protect me from the Plague ...

The music gradually fades away under her speech

At Wothorpe only one nun was left ... the convent closed ... "the pestilence that walketh in darkness—the destruction that wasteth at noonday". These walls, this rough habit—but fine linen next to my skin. These windows, protection against the cold wind. Plain food and the Mother Abbess to guide me. Peace. Peace. A quiet cell. Away from the plague. Prayer. Music. Tending the sick—no—no——no! Oh Lord give me strength. Not the sick. The poor. The poor. Yes. Yes. But not the sick. Scabbed bodies breathing pestilence on a fine mist over us. They will die anyway. Lord save me from the pestilence. Here in my cell I will pray—I will pray day and night for the sick and the wretched. But—I don't want to touch them ... No more riding out at dawn with the mist over the water meadows. My horse stumbling on the rough frozen ground. Cold frosty air. Spiders' webs sparkling with dew. No ... No ... The cloister. The cell. Prayer. Prayer. Holiness. Silence. Away from the sound of my brothers quarrelling. Honest work. And the bell that summons me to prayer.

There is a loud insistent peal at the doorbell. Anna 2 falters

I want—I—I want to——

She goes out quickly

Anna 1 moves into her place. The Lights come up. She stands quite still. The bell peals again and again

She goes out and returns with Daniel, Prue's brother. He is young, ener-getic, self-seeking. His easy charm of manner is highly calculated and he manipulates people shamelessly. He is wearing perfectly anonymous jeans and anorak

Dan You should have asked me for proof of my identity you know.
Anna 1 But—you're Prue's brother.
Dan That's what I said. And you must be Anna. But you shouldn't let strange men into your flat. Not even if they look like policemen! I ought to be carrying a little card with my photo and "Brother of Prunella" stamped on it. I thought there was nobody in by the way. I rang several times.
Anna 1 *(looking round hesitantly)* I was wool-gathering.
Dan Is that more respectable than day-dreaming?
Anna 1 Prue didn't say you'd be here today——
Dan Aah! She did mention me then? ... No. I haven't spoken to Prue for some time. She hasn't given me the go-ahead to be here. I'm trespassing. But my—er—circumstances—altered radically. And I found myself on the street. You look a much softer touch than Prue anyway——
Anna 1 *(drily)* Thanks!
Dan I'm frightened of Prue. She tortured me when I was a child. Then she grew up full of moral certainty. Look! I'm being winsome because I've got nowhere to go. But I can see you're too intelligent to be taken in by my boyish charm. Did you say yes to Prue about me?
Anna 1 Well, yes.

Dan Good. My things are in the hall. Shall I bring them up? There's not much.

Anna 1 I don't want anybody here at the moment really.

Dan Of course you don't. I can see that. You haven't moved in yourself yet, have you? Have you known Prue long?

Anna 1 We were at school together.

Dan So you're a clever girl too!

Anna 1 No. Yes. Why the sneer?

Dan Oh. I'm not sneering. I'm jealous of Prue. My big sister. Did everything right. Prizes every year. Scholarships. Sense of direction. Credit to the family. (*Drily*) An achiever. They sent me to a progressive boarding school when I opted out of being Prue's shadow ... I think Mummy just didn't like having me round the house much ... It was a lovely school. You know, the kind where you strolled in to a maths lesson and said "OK Quentin, you can stuff the calculus. I'm going fishing" ... Lots of nice middle-class girls with terrible legs being as advanced as all get out down by the bike sheds. Have you got any coffee? Beer?

Anna 1 There's some coffee in the kithen. But I'm not waiting on you. Or subsidizing you. You can sleep on this floor and that's that.

Dan Quite right. That's the only way to deal with me. I shall attempt to sponge on you shamelessly. And Prue. I shall enjoy the battle more if you don't give in straight away.

Anna 1 All right then. Convince me why you should stay here tonight when Prue isn't coming till tomorrow.

Dan Prue has a roof over her head. I haven't.

Anna 1 Tough.

Dan I had a room—beautiful it was. Dirt cheap. Very comfortable. Nylon carpet and white melamine. With a very nice landlady. She wasn't like you. She was very stupid. Husband worked for the Gas Board. She kept bringing me offcuts of their dinner because I looked hungry. It was perfect.

Anna 1 Why did you leave?

Dan I cuckolded the man from the Gas Board. That is, I think, the *mot juste*. And he cut up rough. So I left. Hastily.

Anna 1 What do you do? What's your job?

Dan Nothing.

Anna 1 Is Prue supporting you while you're here?

Dan (*smiling*) "You shouldn't make personal remarks. It's very rude." Shouldn't think so. I find all the money I need. Here and there.

Anna 1 (*coldly*) Well, I don't want you staying here very long. This is my room. And I want it to myself. I'm letting you stay as a favour to Prue. I don't like phonies.

Dan (*with a contemptuous grin*) How perceptive you are, dear Anna. Just ignore my attempts as disarming candour. I am quite as shameless as I claim to be but if I tell you first you can't say you haven't been warned.

Anna 1 Get your things.

Dan goes out

After a moment's thought Anna goes to the phone which is on the floor in the corner. She dials

Dan comes in with a rucksack, a bed roll and a string bag of books

(*Acidly*) Thank Christ you haven't got a guitar anyway.
Dan (*sweetly*) I could always get one if you think I should.
Anna 1 Oh hello ... Prue? ... I thought I'd just better tell you ... your brother's turned up. ... Yes, he's bringing it up now. ... I suppose so ... if it really is just for a few days. ... It's all right for me to let him in now then? ... OK. See you. (*She puts the phone down. Grudgingly*) Prue will be here tomorrow. She's a bit fed up with your just turning up like this. You should have waited. You can sleep on this floor. This is my study though and I want it clear during the day. You either get out of the house altogether or you go into Prue's room while she's at the hospital. Keep out of my way. Get your own food and stuff. You can use the kitchen when Prue and I aren't around. I'll work out how much to charge you for gas and hot water. You can have the floor space free. As long as I see very little of you.
Dan "We are the masters now".

Anna looks at him sharply

Anna 1 If you like. (*She tidies up the dirty plates, mugs, bowl of water etc. onto the tray*) I'd rather you didn't touch anything in the kitchen tonight. I've hardly unpacked anything yet. I don't want it messed up before I've sorted it out. The loo's through there. I'm going to bed, Good-night.

She goes out, taking the tray and dirty mugs etc. with her

Dan smiles and whistling gently to himself, begins to unfold his sleeping bag etc., and prepares for bed. But he does not get into bed. He sits cross-legged on his sleeping bag and begins to untie his shoelaces. He smiles and sits quite still. The Lights fade. Music

During the Black-out, Dan exits

The Lights come up again. Dan's sleeping bag is on the floor and his shoes etc. are beside it but Dan is nowhere to be seen. Anna's desk and chair are now onstage, as well as a sofa and coffee table. Music continues to play softly

Anna 1 comes in with a pile of exercise books and a cup of coffee, and a cassette radio. This is the source of the music. Radio 3. Debussy piano music. She puts the books on her chair and switches on the lamp and settles herself at the desk, and begins to glance through the top exercise book

After a moment Prue appears in the doorway

Prue Can I come in?
Anna 1 Yes. I was just summoning up the will to begin this marking. (*She switches off the radio*)

Prue (*looking at the pile*) How many have you got there?
Anna 1 (*smiling*) Twenty-four. "The difficulties encountered by Florence
Nightingale on her arrival at Scutari in the Crimean Campaign."
Prue "Write on one side of the paper only." Sounds like our day ... I
didn't think things were so heavy nowadays.
Anna 1 Don't you start! I am a very old-fashioned teacher. I like sentences.
And writing up to the margins. And "all right" as two words. (*She flips
open a book*) Mind you the gulf between what I want and what I get ...
(*Her voice trails away as she reads. Abstractedly*) This class is one of my
better ones actually ...
Prue Where's Dan?
Anna 1 Haven't seen him today. He'd gone before I was up this morning ...
If you see him you could tell him that if he doesn't clear up in here I
shall chuck his bed in the dustbin.

Pause

Prue Would you rather I told him to go altogether?

Pause

Anna 1 No. Not at the moment anyway.
Prue You don't like him do you?
Anna 1 I don't—care about him either way. I admit I'll be glad when he
goes but that's just because I don't particularly want anyone cluttering
up my room.
Prue I never realized how tidy-minded you were.
Anna 1 (*carefully*) That sounds like a—criticism.
Prue (*off-handedly*) No. Just an observation.

Pause

I don't specially care about my surroundings. So if I get on your nerves
for God's sake, tell me and I'll stop.
Anna 1 That doesn't seem particularly fair.
Prue Well it matters to you. It doesn't to me so I may as well do the
adjusting ... I'm sorry Dan annoys you. (*She gets up and begins to put
away Dan's things in a neat pile*)
Anna 1 Prue! Why are you doing that?
Prue Saves bother.
Anna 1 But why should you wait on Dan?
Prue I don't. But I don't believe in making a fuss over small things. Waste
of energy. I prefer to save mine for the things that matter to me.
Anna 1 But all these little things add up to a sizeable heap.
Prue Yeah sure. I'm not defending my position intellectually. I'm just
saying what I do. (*She grins*) My mother used to drive me crazy when
we were kids. She was forever making a stand on the most trivial issues.
Things that just didn't matter, except for her to win. We'd sit for bloody
hours while she raged on about—oh—putting the lid back on the
marmalade—or whose turn it was to clear the table—till she'd exhausted
herself. I thought then—only fight the battles that matter—and only if

you're going to win. The marmalade stood me in good stead when I decided to be a doctor. Mummy wanted me to be a nurse—much easier and much more suitable. But *I* didn't.

Anna 1 I don't think I could be so—detached.

Prue Is that why you couldn't live with Simon?

Anna 1 Not really. I don't know. Women are supposed to be the emotional ones but some men are so—clinging—mother ... wife, mistress, job, house, car—children. They've got to have them all—just hanging around—to prove they exist.

Prue (*amused*) Like Dan.

Anna 1 Oh, he's just a different sort of parasite. Oh, sorry.

Prue shrugs

Prue Why didn't you move somewhere on your own?

Anna does not reply

Because I won't make emotional demands on you?

Pause

But I do dump my parasitic brother on you, don't I. (*She grins*)

Anna 1 (*slowly*) Friendship is a more—equal relationship.

Prue And you won't feel idealogically threatened if I leave the washing-up to you?

Anna 1 Friendship's a casualty of the way we live isn't it? It doesn't count. Not on its own. With Simon, we weren't even married but we had to be a couple. Friendship by twos. Nick and Claire, Simon and Anna, Richard and Pauline. Put everybody in a box and give them a name. Everybody going on about what they called each other. As if it mattered. My husband. My fella. My boyfriend. My bloke. My live-in lover! This is Ms Wentworth and her paramour. My head of department always called Simon "Your—er—Mr Field". Get into your category and friendship follows like mixed doubles. You stay in your tramlines and I'll stay in mine. "Come round and see us—Oh Simon's away? Never mind ... Come another time when he's back."

Prue (*amused*) Well, you'll step right into another category by moving in with me.

Anna 1 My flatmate. Prue Warren.

Prue Yes. But when it becomes apparent that we are not two fancy-free bachelor girls husband hunting they'll have to fit us into the ladies of Llangollen category.

Anna 1 (*gravely*) OK. You wear the tweed jackets I'll wear the frills.

The bell rings

Prue goes and lets in Dan. He is carrying an old suitcase, and a couple of carrier bags bulging with odds and ends

Dan (*to Prue*) I don't want to worry you but our respected parent is across the road. By the telephone box. Staring up at this house.

Prue Mother? You're joking!
Dan Would that I were. (*To Anna*) Oh! You've made my bed.
Anna 1 No—I——
Dan May I spread my books out here for a little while? (*He begins to unpack several books and range them in piles alongside his bed*)

The phone rings. Prue answers it

Prue Hello? ... Oh, hello, Mother.

Dan collapses with hoots of laughter on to his bed

    (*Gesturing at him to be quiet*) You are? ... Yes of course ... Do you want me to meet you? ... All right then. ... See you. (*She puts the phone down. Delicately*) She's at the station. She's been visiting Lily Cross. Wonders if she could look in on us for a few minutes. ... She doesn't want to be a bother ... I needn't meet her at the station.
Dan Lying old bat. She's outside.
Anna 1 Why the subterfuge?
Dan Mummy is scrupulous about not interfering with our privacy. It's a positive fetish. So she has to resort to the M.I.5 stuff to do simple things like dropping in on Prue's new flat. She didn't even read postcards that came for us when we were kids did she Prue?
Prue. No.
Dan I kept—or rather created—a diary when I was fifteen. It made Frank Harris sound like Benjamin Bunny. I left it lying around half-concealed by my socks and hankies and she never even glanced at it. Outrageous lack of maternal concern. On the evidence of that diary I should have been hauled off to every Child Guidance clinic in the country. I, of course, read everything I can lay my hands on ... I go through peoples' desks too. So if you have any private letters Anna you'd better destroy them. I read that pile of essays last night.
Anna 1 I hope they improved your mind.
Dan Oh yes. They're very informative. And aren't you fierce? You're really determined to be a guiding force in their young lives. Making sure they all look back and say "Miss Wentworth changed my life" ... Do you seduce the boys too?

Anna goes off

    (*Laughing*) She keeps doing that. Gives me a look of silent loathing, and doesn't deign to speak to a toad like me and sweeps out. She spends most of her time in that kitchen.
Prue Watch it. Or you'll find yourself thrown out again.
Dan Oh. You'll protect me won't you, Prunella?
Prue No.
Dan It's just that your little school teacher friend is so very commonplace.
Prue Leave it, Dan.
Dan Who thinks she's so interesting and sensitive I'm surprised you can be bothered with her.
Prue Don't be tiresome Dan.

Dan Do you think she heard me?
Prue Probably. You were speaking loudly enough. When are you leaving?
Dan Soon. Quite soon.

Prue crosses and puts her hands on his shoulders

Prue Don't irritate me Danny boy.

Dan looks directly at her and smiles slightly

Dan No. (*He takes her hand and links little fingers with her. Mocking*) Are you my friend?

The doorbell shrills

Anna 1 looks in the door

Prue (*moving away from Dan; to Anna*) You go. That will be Mummy.

Anna goes out and returns with Harriet Warren. She is a quiet, self-contained woman. Well-dressed and soft-voiced. She is a little nervous at the moment

Harriet I'm dreadfully sorry to intrude like this. But I was visiting an old friend nearby and it seemed a good opportunity to pop in ...

Prue and Dan are silent

Anna 1 It's very nice to see you again, Mrs Warren.
Harriet (*gratefully*) Oh, Anna my dear it must be years. But you haven't changed a bit. You've still got that lovely smile.
Dan And all those—lovely teeth! Hello Mummy! (*He kisses her*)
Harriet I phoned you—at the Locksleys.
Dan I hope you didn't get old man Locksley.
Harriet Yes ... I didn't tell him I was your mother. Hello, Prue.
Prue Hello Mum. Do you want some tea?
Harriet No thank you. I had tea out with Lily.
Dan Oh! You have actually been to Lily's then?
Harriet (*hastily*) I've been staying with her since Friday. Her husband died last week.
Prue Poor old Lily.
Dan And you moved in in a spirit of widowly solidarity?
Anna 1 Won't you sit down Mrs Warren?
Harriet Thank you.
Anna 1 Or would you like to see round the flat?
Dan This is Anna's room really. I'm a squatter.
Harriet Yes. I'd like to (*She does not move*)

Pause

Prue Are you going back to Lily's or are you going home?
Harriet I shall just pick up my things and then go home ... I didn't know you were here, Dan. Mr Locksley told me you'd gone to live with your sister.

Dan No. Just staying for a little while, Mother. Don't upset Anna. She doesn't like me and she's not going to let me clutter up her room much longer.

Harriet I'm glad you're here. I wanted to see you *both*. (*She stresses the word meaningfully*)

There is an awkward pause

Anna 1 Is—is there some private matter? Would you like me to go?

Harriet (*gaily*) Oh no. Nothing at all. I just don't see my children very often. I have to catch them in flight as it were if I want to talk to them. I do apologize for descending on *you* Anna.

Anna 1 Not at all.

Harriet (*off-handedly*) I had to pop in now really because I'm going away for a couple of months actually. So I won't have the opportunity of seeing you for a bit ... I haven't seen you for a while ...

Pause

Prue Where are you going? On holiday?

Harriet I'm going to stay with Beryl and Arthur.

Dan (*softly*) In Johannesburg?

Harriet Yes.

Dan And you've come for a good old liberal workout have you, Mumsie?

Harriet (*evenly*) No. I just came to tell you. (*With a touch of bitterness*) I thought that as I was going for two months you might just notice I wasn't around. And wonder where I was. But I suppose that was a little over-hopeful of me! (*She gets up. More upset than she meant to be*) May I use the bathroom?

Anna 1 Of course.

She leads her out solicitously

Pause

Dan (*very softly*) We are naughty children. Mummy is cross with us.

Prue (*evenly; with no trace of emotion*) Mummy will go away and leave us if we don't behave better.

Anna 1 comes back. She looks at the two of them. She sits at her desk and stares ahead of her. She picks up a pencil and begins to tap it rhythmically on the pile of books on the desk

Anna 1 (*neutrally*) She's crying.

No response from Prue and Dan

The Lights slowly fade

ACT II

The same. A little while later

Anna 1 is sitting at her desk. She is working in a desultory fashion, half-heartedly flipping through the essays on her desk. Her attention is obviously elsewhere. Music. Sweet and remote. Field perhaps or Ravel. She pushes back her chair and leans back with an exercise book in front of her. She begins to read aloud. The music fades

Anna 1 "There is not much point just summing up the difficulties faced by Florence Nightingale in the Crimea. All her life was difficulties. Some of her biggest problems occurred after the Crimean War when she came home. She was a legend in her own lifetime. But there was no room for legends to do anything in England. She took on tasks that were enormous and was not satisfied unless she achieved absolute perfection. If people did not do what she wanted she washed her hands of them. The view of her as the lady with the lamp comforting and being kind is erroneous. Well it was true but not the whole truth. When she first went out to Scutari she wouldn't let her nurses do anything to help the wounded until they were properly asked. They had to be official. She made them wait about until everybody knew they were proper nurses and not just women. She knew what she wanted and went out to get it. Her family were on the whole a major obstacle." (*She laughs and writes something in the book. She looks round worriedly and crosses to the door and listens. She glances at her watch and then returns to her desk and flips idly through the exercise books*)

Prue comes in, she is obviously alive with suppressed anger

Prue Are you working?

Anna shrugs

Can I stay in here for a few minutes? I've shunted Dan off to my room for the time being. He comes out at his peril.
Anna 1 (*carefully*) If you like.

There is an awkward pause. Anna is rather repressive and Prue is restless and angry

Prue (*lightly to conceal her fury*) Mummy has apparently taken root in the bathroom. If you want to use it in the next hour or so we'll have to break the door down.
Anna 1 I see.
Prue Let's assume it's some kind of menopausal dementia. She's never done anything like this before.
Anna 1 Let's assume she's unhappy.
Prue (*shrugging*) There's grandeur!
Anna 1 Oh come on Prue. Don't be childish. She's not the kind of woman to let go like that—in front of me.
Prue Extra leverage. (*She sits down sulkily*)

Anna 1 (*irritably*) Well, you're not just going to sit there! She's desperate. She's locked herself in. She won't answer. Suppose she tries to harm herself.

Prue Think about it. It's a very safe bathroom. What do you think she's going to do? Choke herself to death on the Veeto?

Anna 1 Don't be so cheap.

Prue When Dad died ... she was destroyed—at first. She stumbled her way around in the dark. None of us could touch her. Even if we wanted to. It was awful. Then—imperceptibly—she became the brave little widow "smiling at grief". It was nauseating. She climaxed that stage by cramming down a small handful of aspirin ... just enough to make a dramatic gesture but not enough to finish her off. That way she had all the fun.

Anna 1 But surely——

Prue (*with vicious mockery*) Oh yes. Of course it was a cry for help really. So we all rallied round ... she hadn't enjoyed herself so much for years.

Anna 1 I think you ought to go to her.

Prue Anyway I despise suicides.

Anna 1 (*wistfully*) I'd never have the courage.

Prue (*ungraciously*) Oh grow up. This isn't Five-A debating society ... "This house believes it is more courageous not to throw yourself in front of the Piccadilly Line Tube at Hammersmith."

She looks at Anna. Anna is a little taken aback by Prue's childish reaction to her mother and her coldness irritates Prue further

You go to her if you're so worried. She likes you.

Anna 1 (*wonderingly*) I always envied you your parents when we were at school. Your dad was so good-looking and your mum was such fun. I used to think it was wonderful when you took me back with you after school and said "Oh Mum, Anna's stopping for tea. OK?" And she always used to say "Of course darling. How lovely" ... And you had a record-player and floor cushions in your room ... My mum needed three weeks' notice to change her cardigan.

Prue She was all right ... Quite restful really.

Anna 1 I used to pray she wouldn't come to school for anything. I didn't tell her most things that happened. I used to shove the letters about Open Day down the side of the sofa until it was over then find it and pretend to be upset. I always thought she looked like my grandma ... She was forty-one when I was born ... stayed at home till she was thirty-nine looking after her dad. Then he died and she married Dad quick. I don't think he meant to marry her. He was just passing the time of day with that nice Miss Springett that had been so good to her dad. Then there he was married—with a lovely little girl who was a real credit to them. They idolized me. Still do ... (*She sighs*)

Prue Which is why you've put two hundred miles between you.

There is a pause

Anna 1 (*painfully*) Prue ... I don't want to ... talk to your mother ... but I think you ought to do something about her.

Prue Like euthanasia you mean?
Anna 1 Please don't be flippant. She's here. She's unhappy. You can't just ignore her.
Prue I can and will.
Anna 1 I never realized you were so callous.
Prue (*quietly*) I won't submit to emotional blackmail. She'll come out when she's ready ... I have itemized—in my mind—the contents of the bathroom, and unless she chooses to drown herself there is nothing she can hurt herself with. You can hear that Ascot in High Wycombe so we know she hasn't run any water.
Anna 1 What's she got with her?

Pause. Prue does not answer

Well?
Prue I don't know! She's in there crying. Laughing. Reading *Spare Rib.* Plucking her eyebrows or tinting her hair. Whatever she's doing it's her business. She will stop when she's ready and it's up to her to decide when to come out ... If she's cut herself I'll put a plaster on it for her but I won't be drawn into her tacky little emotional game.
Anna 1 And Dan?
Prue He'll make her come out when he wants to pee.
Anna 1 And if not?
Prue (*grinning*) No. He'd probably pee in the waste-paper basket in my room now you come to think of it.

Anna turns away. Prue watches her ruefully

Do you know a good desert island where you don't have to have eight gramophone records, the Bible and Shakespeare? "And what about your luxury Dr Warren?" (*Savagely*) "No people!"

Prue goes out

Anna turns back and stares after her. She crosses to the sofa and sits, defeated. She stiffens irritably and reaches behind her. One of Dan's books was there half-concealed by the cushion. She looks at it for a moment, is about to drop it behind the sofa with the rest of Dan's belongings. Then very deliberately, she tears out several pages and rips them across. She yanks the remaining pages away from the spine and throws the lot behind the sofa with spiteful pleasure. She bends down and crosses her arms on her lap and buries her face

Music. Remote. Eerie. The Lights fade leaving a pool of light near Anna's desk

Anna 2 enters. She is wearing Victorian clothes, a long cloak wrapped over a drab grey dress. She passes her hand wearily over her forehead

Anna 2 That was the worst of it. Not to be able to do anything. It was a denial of our humanity somehow. But Miss Nightingale was adamant. We were not to lift a finger until the doctors asked us to. Otherwise we would be just another rabble of women wanting to help and getting in the way. Fine ladies in self-consciously simple clothes—made for the occasion—offering sal volatile to a man whose stomach has been shot away. Or dirty drabs in indecent rags offering cheap gin and whorish comforts because that is all they have ... The filth. The flies and the stink ... They jeered at us when we set to to clean it up ... but that was women's work, that was all right. But then when the casualties began to come in ... more died of dysentery and cholera than wounds ... but we still stood there. Till they asked us to help—acknowledged us—we did not exist ... A boy lying on a stretcher at my feet, his tongue cracked, his face a filthy mask of smoke and blood, his eyes beseeching me for help ... his leg a bloody stump crawling with maggots! And I turned away. All he wanted was someone to show some care, a little cool water on his forehead. His eyes were already glazing over. His blood was black and sticky and he couldn't move to brush away those terrible gorged flies ... And we waited. We were to be nurses, not angels with welling eyes delicately wiping way a little blood with a lace trimmed handkerchief. But it was hard. (*This last is spoken with a fierce quiet pain*) Hard to do the right thing when it doesn't seem to be the human thing ... the faces the eyes ... the hands reaching—— (*She stops leaving the words hanging in the air as her thoughts go inward*)

The music ends. The Lights come up over the whole stage

Anna 2 sidles quietly away

Dan enters breezily

Dan Mother has vacated the bathroom and is recovering her equilibrium in the kitchen. She will join us for tea and she will not cry any more. Were you asleep?

Anna 1 No. (*She gets up quickly and crosses back to her desk. She begins to stack the exercise books together*) I was *trying* to work!

Dan grins. Anna 1 slams the pile of exercise books down ferociously on the desk. One of the books flies to the floor. Dan picks it up with a flourish. He opens it and reads silently for a moment. Then grins. Anna who has been holding out her hand for the book, sighs, sits down resting her forehead on her hand, hiding her eyes

Dan Ho. Ho. This is inflammatory stuff. "Florence Nightingale did not like women much. Especially stupid women. She got fed up with ladies playing at nurses. She once wrote 'The women have made no improvement, they have only tried to be "men" and they have succeeded only in being "third rate men".' She did not do this herself of course." (*He looks at the name on the front of the book*) Tracy Fielding. Good old Tracy! I think you should make a sampler of that beautiful sentiment, Anna, and put it over your bed ... You've only given Tracy B-minus. Is that for not toeing the Party Line. "All women are wise and wonderful at all times and do wise and wonderful things. And when they don't do wise and wonderful things, which we don't admit, we don't refer to that because it isn't wise and wonderful ever to criticize our sisters!"

Anna 1 ignores him

Anna! Aren't you going to fix me with a basilisk stare and strike me
down for being unreconstructed?

Anna 1 sits quite still

Anna 1 There's nothing sillier than arguing with someone who doesn't
care tuppence about what matters to you. It's no contest.
Dan Oh. Aren't you going to win me over? "There is more joy in Heaven
over one sinner", you know.
Anna 1 You don't care enough about anything to be either a sinner or
repentant.
Dan Oh I do! I care passionately about me!
Anna 1 (*with a slight laugh*) Ye-es!
Dan (*softly*) I don't believe in changing the system. Just playing it.
Anna 1 (*sadly*) Probably all comes to the same thing in the end. I had a
friend who used to say "In a hundred years' time this problem will have
ceased to exist so why get worked up about it now?"
Dan Exactly.
Anna 1 I can't do that though.
Dan That's because you're a true Romantic—"One to whom the agonies
of the world *are* agonies and will not let them rest." Keats. Yes? Oh no.
You teach History don't you?
Anna 1 It's better than being a parasite posing as a latter-day Nihilist.
Dan (*with a grin; delighted*) Nothing so political. I'm just psychologically
debilitated by my sister's moral energy. Daddy was a doctor too you
know. It was me that was supposed to follow in his footsteps not Prue,
but the lines got crossed. He died a disappointed man—in me you
understand not Prue! Mummy loves me though. (*Smugly*) Women always like their sons best you know. There's a special bond. (*Mocking*)
Especially emancipated ladies or so my observations tell me.
Anna 1 (*acidly*) Doting on the runt of the litter instead of abandoning it—
like all sensible animals.
Dan (*with an odd amused seriousness*) You won't make it, Anna. You'd
like to be a hard-liner but deep down you're fatally—(*he looks appraisingly at her*)—wishy-washy! You don't know where you want to go and
you don't know how to get there. Twentieth-Century Woman's dilemma!
Anna 1 And where do you want to go?
Dan (*grinning*) I'm just going to be where it's *comfy!* (*Stretching*) It's about
time someone plied me with tea and cakes while we're on the subject of
my well-being.
Anna 1 Is your mother all right?
Dan Oh yes. There's no need for you to fuss round her. It's me you should
be ministering to. Mummy's in the kitchen trying to get a kind word
out of Prue ... People always want what they can't get. I've got lots of
kind words but she's not bothered. I'm kind to animals and children
and cripples and the Old. Much less effort than being beastly. Do you

know. ("*Patience Strong*" *voice*) I read on the back of a match box that it takes seven muscles to smile but forty-two to frown. Isn't that a wonderful human thought?

Anna 1 Oh piss off: (*She is irritated beyond measure*)

Dan You don't mean that.

Anna 1 Yes I do! That's exactly what I mean ... I don't have to have you here cluttering up my flat, making a nuisance of yourself, driving me crazy!! You—you'd better make some other arrangements. I'd rather you went.

Dan I'll tell Prue. She's awfully fair-minded. She won't let you bully me.

Anna 1 makes a noise of inarticulate rage and pushes aside the sofa, which has been concealing Dan's belongings.

Anna 1 Just clear out. And you can clear that rubbish out. I won't have you or your belongings cluttering up my room a moment longer. I am sick and tired of the whole damn thing.

Dan gets up slowly and wanders over to Anna. He looks at her disdainfully as if her outburst of rage was what he was hoping for

Dan Poor Anna. Can't cope. Tschk. Tschk. (*He bends down lazily to pick up his books and sees the torn-up book. He stays quite still, on one knee, not touching the book*) Did you do that?

Anna has forgotten. She stares at the torn-up book for a moment as if she has no idea how it got there. There is a sudden tension in the air

Anna 1 Oh—(*Defiantly*) Yes, I did.

Dan That was very naughty. (*Silkily*) You shouldn't have done that.

Anna 1 turns away

Anna 1 I was—angry.

Dan I think you ought to pick it up.

His voice is very quiet and unemphatic but there is an air of danger about him. Anna is confused, a little afraid like a defiant child who knows that she ʽₐₛ done wrong but can't bring herself to admit it or apologize

(*Sweetly*) Anna. Did you hear what I said?

Anna 1 I'm sorry—(*She stops, unable to continue*)

Dan Pick it up.

Anna 1 No.

Dan (*sighing*) Oh dear.

He crosses to Anna and stands very close looking down at her. Her head is bowed

Do as I tell you.

He takes hold of her wrist. Anna stiffens and makes as if to pull away then realizes that to struggle would be a waste of time and stands quite still

Very wise. Are you going to pick it up?

Anna 1 Let go my wrist.

Dan shakes his head

Dan Do as you're told.

He twists her arm behind her back and catches her other wrist as she raises a hand to hit him. He takes both wrists behind her back turning her round and forces her down towards the floor beside the book

Anna 1 You're hurting my wrists.
Dan Yes.

He pushes her further down. She is on the floor and he is kneeling beside her. She is quite unable to move. Suddenly he lets her go and stands up

(*Brightly*) OK. Let's leave it there.

Anna gets to her feet. She is angry and humiliated and upset but determined not to show it

I shall be going soon. I couldn't stay in a home with so little regard for literature. (*He crosses quickly to Anna, takes her hand raises it very quickly and kisses her wrist*) Don't pretend. I didn't hurt you very much.
Anna 1 It's what I'd expect from you. Cheap violence.

Dan finds this irresistibly funny and hoots with laughter

Dan At least you had the sense not to come at me with your little fists flailing! I don't hold with violence—far too exhausting ... but you'd be very unwise to leave it out of your sisterly calculations.

Anna turns away in contempt

We civilized beings can have a gentlemen's agreement about it but it's always an option. What are you going to do about it? Put flowers round my neck and sing to me?
Anna 1 I despise you.
Dan So you should. But contempt isn't going to change anything is it?

Prue comes in

Prue She's all right now. She would like some tea after all.
Anna 1 (*hastily*) I'll see to it. Does she want something to eat?
Prue I've put the kettle on. Biscuits'll do. Don't make her feel too welcome.
Dan What she's really come for is a lovely emotional workout. Loves a nice scene does Mummy. She wants us to denounce her for going to South Africa then she can justify herself with throbbing appeals to our sense of family loyalty.
Prue (*with distaste*) Beryl's her sister.
Dan And Arthur has all the compassion and sensitivity you would expect from someone who fled post-war Britain to find the Earthly Paradise in South Africa.
Prue Mum won't buy Outspan oranges on moral grounds, but Beryl and

Arthur are family! ... We have a lovely cousin too. Tony. He's really lovable! When they came over here a few years ago he told us how he ran a "Kaffir" down in his sports car and made a nasty dent in the bonnet!

Dan I poured a bowl of vegetable soup over his head. I told him it wasn't on purely political grounds. He was a prick anyway. Caused a nasty rift. He sat there with bits of diced carrot plopping into his lap while Arthur raged about the Communist menace ... I was very young of course. That was in my activist phase. I've eschewed violence since then. (*With a grin at Anna*) By and large. Indeed action of any kind! So you see Mummy has actually come here for our forgiveness and our blessing.

Anna looks profoundly depressed

Prue Don't worry, Anna. We'll get rid of her. Dan's exaggerating.

Anna 1 I don't want you to get rid of her ...

Prue Yes you do, love. (*She smiles wanly at Anna*) This isn't what you meant at all is it?

Anna 1 No it isn't ... Simon's looking in later! (*She begins to giggle*)

Dan Aah! The discarded suitor! I shall enjoy meeting him. Shall I tell him that you and I no sooner looked but loved and he might as well sod off?

Anna 1 No.

Harriet returns. She is quite composed

I'm just going to make some tea, Mrs Warren. Do you like China or Indian?

Harriet Oh, China would be lovely thank you.

Dan And cucumber sandwiches.

Anna 1 There'll be some hot water left in the kettle. You can make yourself some instant coffee—if you've got any.

Dan blows her a kiss

Anna 1 goes out

Prue (*to Harriet*) When are you going? To Johannesburg, I mean ...

Harriet The end of the month. I'll be back in December. Mrs Harris next door is going to keep an eye on the house for me.

Dan There's no need. I'll move in while you're away.

Harriet Oh ... Well I'm not sure I can trust you on your own.

Dan (*conspiratorially*) The neighbours you mean? Don't worry, I'll be very circumspect. A positive Boy Scout—dripping with purity and self-sufficiency.

Harriet Well, I suppose——

Dan Anyway darling, I've got a key so there's nothing you can do about it. Except get the locks changed before you go and that would seem to be a bit excessive. And I do know how to jiggle the bathroom window to climb in if you remember.

Anna 1 comes in with a tray of tea, biscuits, etc.

You'd be doing Anna a favour too. She's dying to get rid of me. Aren't you dear?

Anna 1 Yes. Milk or lemon, Mrs Warren.

Harriet Milk please.

Anna pours some tea and hands her a cup. She then gives some to Prue during the next exchanges. Then Dan

Dan Goodness how cosy! The logs crackling in the grate. The cat asleep on the rug in front of the fire. The lamplight catching Anna's hair as she bends over her sewing. The only sound the rustling as Prue turns over the pages as she sits curled up in her chair, absorbed in her book. Mother, her busy hands stilled, has allowed her knitting to drop into her lap and her eyes have gently closed as she dozes in the firelight. And Dan reflectively bites into a toasted muffin as he thinks over the events of the day ... Outside the wind rattles the chimney pots and shakes the last few leaves from the trees. The acrid smell of smoke hangs in the air, outside the burning leaves in the square. Tea-time in an English home at peace with itself!

Harriet (*quietly*) Don't bother, Daniel. I was listening outside the door. I heard what you said about me.

Dan (*quietly*) That was very naughty of you.

Harriet I'm no longer very interested in your—fanciful explanations of my behaviour ... I don't care what you and Prunella think about my going to South Africa. I simply thought that you should know that I was going. How long I was going to be and when I would be returning.

Dan (*silkily*) Oh dear. Daniel and Prunella. We are in the doghouse.

Harriet I would rather you didn't patronize me, but I suppose it's too late to expect you to change.

Her icy self-control hides a deep hurt which they are aware of

It's something I've never done before as far as I remember—eavesdropping. I'm sorry you regard me with such contempt.

Prue (*quickly*) I'm sorry, Mum. We were—(*looking for the right word. With some self-loathing*)—showing off!

Harriet (*flatly*) Beryl has cancer.

Pause

Dan Game, set and match to Mummy! (*Softly*) If you believe that circumstances alter cases! Poor old Auntie Beryl. Won't she be coming back here for some treatment on the National Health? Arthur's not one to chuck away good money on lost causes.

The doorbell rings

Anna 1 Simon!

She goes out

Harriet Would you pour me some more tea please, Prue? I must be going in a minute.

Prue crosses to her mother. They stare bleakly at one another for a moment

Anna returns with Simon

Dan Hello Simon. You don't know me. I'm Dan, Prue's brother. This is Harriet our mother. We're all imposing on Anna. But we'll go away in a minute. So as not to interrupt your tête-à-tête. Tea? China or Indian?

Simon Hello, Prue. How do you do, Mrs Warren?

Prue I'll put some more water in the pot.

She has picked up the teapot and is looking inside it. There is a moment's awkward pause. She goes out

Anna 1 Sit down, Simon.

He does so, glancing at Dan's belongings behind the sofa

Dan Mine. I'm staying here. Anna has graciously leased me six feet of floor space. She'd rather lease me six feet of newly-dug grave but her liberal conscience prevents her from admitting that openly.

Anna 1 (*evenly*) No it doesn't. Not after a week's acquaintance.

Dan (*chattily to Simon*) This hostility is assumed, you understand to conceal her guilty awareness of my sexual magnetism.

Anna 1 You can do better than that, Dan. That's the oldest fantasy in the book. Don't waste your time complicating the issue. I don't like you. I wish you'd go away.

Dan Slow fade. Music. Fade in the bedroom. Dark brown sheets to signify sophistication. Hi-fi by the bed. Anna. Hair tumbled about her face. Naked beneath the duvet. Dan beside her. Happy satiety. Fade out. It's an attractive prospect.

Anna 1 About as attractive as having your toenails pulled out one by one.

Prue returns with the teapot

Anna sits at her desk. Dan is standing in Prue's way

Prue 'Scuse me Dan.

Dan Oh sorry.

He moves away upstage and watches quizzically as Prue begins to pour some tea for Simon.

Quite a party isn't it? Do we get balloons when we go?

The Lights fade leaving a spot on Anna 1. The others move to the sides of the set and are backlit so that we have four silhouettes motionless

Anna 2 comes into the centre of the stage and the light plays on her face

We see the two Annas brightly lit with the blank figures of the others symmetrically around them

Anna 2 I keep having the same dream—nightmare I suppose. I am in a sunlit room. It's very quiet. Afternoon. Very beautiful. There's a tree outside the window and the sun shines through the leaves and makes lovely dancing patterns on the wall. I'm sitting in a big—velvet—arm-chair reading. There's a baby's cot. Pretty. Frilly. A wicker cot with a froth of frills and pink ribbons. The baby is asleep and the birds are singing outside. There's a lot of them on the lawn—that noisy fighting over food they do about teatime—have you noticed? It's one of those windy days ... bright sun and a warm gusty wind. Autumn I think because the light is soft and golden. The baby wakes up and I pick it up and it laughs and gurgles at me. I take it out into the garden to see the birds. It must have been raining earlier because the grass is wet and the birds are going crazy pulling up worms. But when I look they're not worms—they're fingers. The birds are getting hold of the fingers and pulling and whole hands are coming up and twisting and writhing. The grass is just a mass of grasping hands all reaching out and slithering like snakes. I am terrified and try to step between them but there are so many and they all reach out for me. And—I—put the baby down. And I know that I shouldn't. And the hands drag it through the earth—like worms with a bit of leaf. Then there's nothing—just the lawn—and I have to keep searching. But I can't find the place where the baby went. And everything is quite—quite silent.

The Lights change, flashing eerily across the stage. Anna 2 crosses round by the other four people on the stage. They stretch out their hands to her, trying to touch her. She goes towards them but draws back and away avoiding their touch. Music. Which has begun softly during this reaches a scream

   Black-out, during which all go out

The Lights come up again on an empty stage

   Prue comes in with Simon

Prue You'd better sit down for a minute. Anna's in the bath. I'll tell her you're here.

   She goes off

Simon sits down. Picks up a paper. Puts it down again. He is obviously ill at ease

   Prue comes back

She won't be long.
Simon Oh—good.
Prue (*drily*) She wasn't expecting you.
Simon No.
Prue She's not best pleased you're here.
Simon No. I don't suppose she is.
Prue Just thought I'd warn you.

Pause. Prue seems about to go. Then stops

   (*Not unkindly*) You do haunt us a bit you know, Simon.
Simon Yes. I know.

Prue It—irritates Anna.

Simon Does it irritate you?

Prue No. I don't irritate easy. Anyway, having inflicted my mum and my baby brother on Anna I can hardly object to you padding about the place like a faithful hound.

Simon (*smiling*) Is that what I'm like?

Prue Well. Let's say I never understood the expression doggy devotion till I met you.

Simon I don't see any point in pretending to be something I'm not.

Prue In your case, that could be counter-productive.

Simon You're surely not suggesting I play the masterful hero? Stride in here. Sweep all her belongings into the waste-paper basket and rush her out to my waiting car for a headlong rush through the night to an unknown destination?

Prue Hello nineteen twenty-five! You'd never make it. Anyway, it might be what she'd like deep down—I suspect it might be!—but she's developed such a good network of surface desires she'd cripple you.

Pause

Simon That sounds as if you despise her.

Prue (*surprised*) Good God no! Why do you say that?

Simon You talk about her in such a dismissive manner. (*Tartly*) I suppose that's your scientific detachment!

Prue Ah shit! Scientific detachment! What you see is the detachment of Prunella Warren. Don't be so—blinkered. I'd be detached, as you call it, if I were a farmer's wife up to my knees in mud and cowdung with seven apple-cheeked kids frolicking round me. I am me. I do what I do. Anna is Anna. Let's not fudge everything up with stereotypes!

Simon If you can believe it's that simple.

Prue I am very fond of—I like—I love Anna. There aren't actually any words for my feelings. Very strong. Very caring. Ugh! I'd like to be able to say Anna and I are friends and have it understood. I haven't any romantic illusions about Anna like you have. It may sound pompous but my friendship with her is based on a knowledge of what she's really like! It's pretty obvious but nobody seems to believe it. Friendship between women doesn't have to be defined by their relationships to men. Nobody's threatening you. So for God's sake stop persecuting Anna with your dogginess!

There is an almost comic ferocity in her tone. Simon smiles

Simon You took Anna away for whatever reason.

Prue She went! You should come and talk to some of my patients. Ordinary. Down to earth women. With husbands and kids ... screaming for Valium if they haven't got any friends. "I'm on my own. Shut up all day with the kids. Nobody to talk to. Nobody to understand." A girlfriend to have coffee and a natter with about things you don't talk to your husband about makes a hell of a difference!

Simon (*contemptuously*) So friendship between women can solve all the social evils of our time can it?

Prue No. That's not what I said. But it would be a start if you admitted its existence. Come on, Simon you'd be just as peeved if you shared a flat with one of your friends and everybody immediately said, "Oh, I didn't know he was gay!" Dumping people into categories all the time! "Attractive thirty-two year old blue-eyed blonde (thirty-four, twenty-six, thirty-six) constant companion of debonair man-about-town (forty-two) said 'We are just good friends.'" Where's the difference? Friendship between men and women could do with an airing too!

Simon So you think I ought to go away and leave Anna alone?

Prue I don't know. (*Going*) You're a separate area of Anna's existence. Nothing to do with me.

Simon I love Anna. I want to marry her.

Prue stops. Stands and looks at him. Then expels her breath

Prue (*ruefully*) Christ Almighty! (*Ironically*) That's asking a bit much ... Why? Marriage I mean?

Simon (*bitterly*) Because I'm a dinosaur ... I like the idea of commitment ... fidelity ... children.

Anna comes in, a towel round her head. She is drying her hair. She glances incuriously at the other two, who register without acknowledging her presence

Prue Oh. There's no answer to that!

Simon (*glancing at Anna*) While you're sorting out the stereotypes, Prue, spare a thought for the poor hapless male who likes the idea of paternity ... If you want to play Mothers and Fathers these days it's getting increasingly hard to find a Mother who'll let you join in.

Prue laughs

Anna 1 Fair declaration of intent. Hello Simon.

Simon True. "Now young man, are your intentions strictly dishonourable? Will you promise to love my daughter and leave her? Go halves on the cost of the abortion and omit to love, honour and cherish her because that would be an act of oppression."

Anna 1 (*acidly*) Till *death* do you part!

Simon (*carefully*) That was fairly cheap, Anna.

Pause

Anna 1 (*very quietly*) No ... it wasn't. It was worse than that. I forgot.

She goes out

Simon That makes it pretty clear ... I won't stay now. Say goodbye to Anna for me. Good-night Prue.

He goes out

Prue And good-night to you too! (*She sits moodily*) OK, Anna! He's gone. You can come out now!

Anna 1 returns. She remains upstage

He says goodbye. Do you want me to shout goodbye from you to him out of the window?

Anna 1 No.

Prue Twitchy sort of fellow your Simon ... Well, I need cheering up! I think I'll go and read *The Lower Depths.*

Anna 1 I'm very sorry you had to cope with Simon. I didn't ask him round.

Prue I don't mind Simon. It's the pair of you together I can't stand.

Anna 1 No ... That was my fault. I could have bitten my tongue out ... Simon——

She stops as if wondering whether to go on or not. There is a pause during which she seems to be trying to find the right thing to say. She draws in her breath, and expels it in a rather hopeless sigh. Prue looks enquiringly at her. Anna shakes her head slightly

Nothing ...

The Lights fade to a pool of light c. *Anna 1 and Prue freeze. Music—the Wedding March by Mendelssohn played quietly on a piano—continues throughout the following sequence*

Anna 2 and Simon enter very formally from opposite sides of the stage and meet and stand facing each other

Simon is wearing a dark suit and has a white carnation in his buttonhole. He is holding a grey top-hat. Anna 2 is wearing a wedding dress. White lacy, "ballerina" length. She has white stockings and white high-heeled shoes. She is wearing wrist-length white gloves and a little pearl head-dress with a short bouffant veil. She is carrying a spray of flowers. (Arum lilies if possible, but predominantly white flowers must make up the bouquet.) The veil is covering her face

(Simon's voice) Dearly beloved we are gathered here today ... etc.

Anna 2 and Simon slowly turn and stand facing out front side by side as if at the altar. The voice-over fades and returns, odd sentences from the marriage service being audible

(Very clearly) 'Do you Valerie Elizabeth, take this man, Simon James Henry to be your lawful wedded husband ... *etc.*

Anna 2 No. I am Anna. My name is Anna.

She puts back her veil revealing her face. The voice continues. Anna 2 turns and begins to go. Simon catches her wrist and holds her still

Voice ... forsaking all other as long as you both shall live ... Those whom God hath joined together let no man put asunder.

The music becomes louder in a burst—the orchestral version of the Wedding March, very loud and cheerful. Simon tucks Anna 2's hand in his arm and leads her forward. Bride and Groom processing from the church to face the photographers. During the following speech at orchestrated moments Simon and Anna 2—guided by Simon—pose in traditional poses as if for the wedding album—Simon smiling down at her; both of them looking back over their shoulders at the camera; Anna bending down as if accepting a lucky horseshoe; looking into each other's eyes; laughing at something out of sight etc. Anna 2 is a mechanical doll during these poses. Simon speaks energetically, pausing when necessary for the 'photographs'. (Perhaps flash and the clicking of cameras?)

Simon Everyone agreed it was a beautiful wedding. "The bride looked radiant" ... I'll show you the photographs sometime—she didn't actually, but never mind ... Oh we were wonderfully happy ... But in the pictures there's this thin anxious girl, peering a bit. She was short-sighted and she wasn't wearing her glasses. Dressed in a madly elaborate piece of fancy dress ... Great big white crinoline affair, and her hair piled up in a sort of pearly coronet. Me in a morning suit holding the topper because there was no way I was ever going to put it on my head. Val's friends from school—two of them—in full-length bronze coloured dresses that would come in handy afterwards for parties ... We went to a lot of parties in those days, where girls wore bronze dresses and little gold sandals and laquered hair. Everybody dressed up. Making a statement. This is a big day. Marriage must not only be done it must be seen to be done. We have put all these clothes on—which don't fit us comfortably—and we're all going to drink champagne and eat vol-au-vents and make set speeches in a set pattern. And Val and Simon are going to pose smilingly with a large knife held over an elaborate, ludicrous wedding cake. Then they will change out of these clothes and put on others equally assumed. And we will throw torn-up bits of coloured paper at, them and they will ride off in a large expensive car, festooned with old shoes and tin cans, to a ritual defloration in a luxury hotel.

The music stops. Anna 2 puts her hands over her ears and bends away. Simon steps aside, smiling, leaving Anna 2 to face the camera for the pictures of the bride alone. Mechanically she allows herself to be posed, Simon placing her flowers, her veil etc. He watches indulgently as she is "photographed"

It's the feeling that everything was incomplete. She was fifteen when I first met her. I was eighteen. We got engaged when she was nineteen. Married a year later ... It seemed like an affirmation of something at the time. We were very young—and very conformist too I suppose.

Anna 2 stands quite still. Her hands by her sides. Her bouquet brushing the floor. Simon is quite still

And six years later Val was dead. Suddenly. Appallingly. And our—wedding—just became part of the waste of it all. Waste of money spending all that on a wedding when the bride doesn't make it to her tenth wedding anniversary! ... All that time and energy wasted by her mother when she was little ... worrying about her eating too many sweets and ruining her teeth ... worrying about her O levels ...

Worrying about her staying out after ten-thirty ... And Val and me ... buying our little house ... bickering over the decorations ... beginning to wonder why she didn't get pregnant. Twenty-six years of wasted effort. If we'd known she was going to die we needn't have bothered about anything. Doesn't matter if she gets whooping cough, Mrs Hastings, she's going to die ... Don't bother to have a sperm count Mr Field—corpses don't conceive.

As he speaks Anna 2 slowly takes off her gloves and veil and drops them on to the floor. The veil flutters down at her feet. She places her flowers on the veil. She stands quite still alone in the light, her eyes closed. Black-out

During the Black-out, Simon and Anna 2 exit, taking the flowers etc. with them

The Lights come up on Prue and Anna 1 in the same positions they were in at the beginning of the wedding sequence. There is a slight pause. Prue looks questioningly at Anna 1

Prue Yes?

Anna 1 Nothing. (*She gets up resolutely as if to change the subject but stops and looks directly at Prue. She speaks briskly and unemotionally*) Simon was married before and his wife died. She was only twenty-six—or something. And I forgot. It just didn't cross my mind.

Prue nods her head slightly as if everything had become clear to her

Prue What was it—cancer?

Anna 1 No. Some sort of kidney disease I think. I'm not sure. He never mentions her ... That's why I forgot. No it's not.

Prue And he wants to marry you to prove he's not a failure as a husband. A sense of responsibility's all very well but you can't take the blame for your wife's kidneys packing it in.

Anna 1 I don't honestly know. Simon's very—(*she searches for the right word*)—reticent.

Prue Well, that's better than those ghastly leeches who give you an intimate account of their emotional career from playgroup onwards. Then three days later you hear them going through the same traumatic tale in the same words with the same broken sobs and agonized pauses.

Anna 1 (*amused*) You won't be specializing in psychiatry then?

Prue (*laughing as she stretches*) Nope! Broken bones and elusive viruses that's me. Oh I'll grant you the other side of it but include me out!

Anna 1 No. To be fair Simon's not like that ... It's not self-pity with him—he takes a long time to trust people and then trusts them all in a heap.

Prue Foolish Simon!

Anna 1 Yes. I think he—(*she holds up her hands in despair at the word*)—loves me. But what's the point? I don't—you can't—stick with somebody just because they're suitable ... you like them and feel sorry for them.

Prue There's nothing more intractable than a one-sided relationship ... Thank God Mummy brought Dan and me up to be emotional cripples!

Anna 1 (*quickly*) That's not true!

Prue No. Eunuchs perhaps ... metaphorically speaking!
Anna 1 There's nothing I can do about Simon. His needs are his own
affair, I'm afraid ... It's like those pathetic kids who want to be liked.
There's a girl in the fourth-year group I take ... Absolutely standard
case ... ludicrously so. One-parent family. Mother a bit of a drink
problem ... She longs so painfully to be popular. It hurts to see her with
the other girls ... She crawls ... none of it works ... The awful thing is
she's horribly hard to like.
Prue Well ... wouldn't do if we were all alike would it ... as they say.
Blood. Bones. Tissue. Nerves. Too many variations on the basic model.

The doorbell rings

Is that Simon back?

Anna 1 shrugs and goes to the door. She returns with Harriet

Mother! Come in. You're very welcome!

Harriet looks sharply at her

No I mean it. What do you want?
Harriet I've come for Dan's things.
Prue Why can't he fetch them himself?
Anna 1 You mean he's leaving?

Prue laughs

Prue Don't be so eager, Anna. Dan has a nasty habit of returning—as it
were—to his vomit!
Anna 1 Oh please God no!
Harriet He has moved into my house.
Prue Oh, Mummy, Mummy! It used to be our home!
Harriet While I'm away, Prue, can you make sure he doesn't wreck the
place?
Prue Oh come on Mum, that won't be necessary. He's too lazy for any-
thing but emotional destruction.
Harriet I'd rather not take the risk ... Would you like to use my car while
I'm away? I don't want Daniel using it.
Prue You've gone off Dan in a big way suddenly.
Harriet Don't be silly. I just have a healthy respect for my own property.
Prue OK. Thanks. Yes. The car would be fine. What happens if *I* wrap it
round a lamp post?
Harriet I don't think that's very likely.
Anna 1 Why isn't Dan collecting his own stuff?
Harriet Pure laziness. He knew I was coming over here. I've cancelled the
papers, had the central heating serviced ... stopped the milk and so on,
so there shouldn't be any trouble.
Prue (*amused*) Have you had locks put on the telephone?
Harriet Dan waits for people to phone him.

Prue goes behind the sofa and pulls out Dan's belongings

Prue There's his washing-kit in the bathroom isn't there?

She goes out. The atmosphere is frosty

Anna 1 Do sit down, Mrs Warren.
Harriet You're beautifully polite, Anna ... You must have found Daniel a terrible strain ...
Anna 1 No. Just—a gadfly.

Prue returns with a sponge bag which she packs away in Dan's rucksack

Prue There we are.
Anna 1 I don't see why he couldn't see to them himself.
Prue Oh it would have driven you crazy. This would have sat in that corner for months. Dan's a master of the old leave-it-long-enough-and-somebody-else-will-do-it trick!
Harriet And you've always fallen for it. When you were children and I sent you up to tidy your rooms you'd get yours done in half an hour. Dan would lie on his bed reading, then pick up a couple of bits of paper and whine that he was exhausted—and you used to creep in and do it for him. (*She laughs silently, attempting to ingratiate herself with Prue*)
Prue (*irritably*) Well, it used to drive me crazy ... You locked him up there every Sunday ... We had those awful scenes and it was perfectly obvious that he wasn't going to do anything.
Harriet Very bad for his character. He was always a selfish little boy.
Prue I never did believe in cursing the darkness—not when I had the candle and the matches in my hand. And the lights had fused ...
Harriet (*coldly*) Practical Prue! Is that why you've given me such short shrift about my trip?
Prue (*levelly*) Nothing's going to stop you going is it? ... Discussing it would be an indulgence.

Harriet stares at her daughter unsure of what to say next. The phone rings

Excuse me. (*She crosses and picks up the phone*) Prue Warren ... Yes ... Mm ... I see ... Yes ... I'll be right over. (*She puts down the phone and smiles almost triumphantly at her mother*) That was the hospital ... I'm on call ... I don't know when I'll be back ... Can you manage that? (*Indicating Dan's belongings*)
Anna 1 I'll see to it.
Prue See you.

She goes out very fast

Harriet (*slowly to herself*) I wonder ...

Harriet crosses to the window and stares out. Anna 1 looks helplessly at her

Anna 1 Would you like some coffee—or shall I take these down to the car for you?
Harriet (*not looking at her*) Mmm? Oh. No thank you.

Anna 1 raises her eyes heaven-wards

There she goes ... Practically running away from me ... I don't suppose she's really going to the hospital is she?
Anna 1 (*surprised*) Well, yes! Of course she is! What else would that be? (*Gesturing to the phone*)

Harriet slowly comes away from the window

Harriet Yes. I suppose so ... I could have given her a lift. (*She shifts Dan's rucksack slightly with her foot*)
Anna 1 Do you want to stay? Or shall I help you with that?
Harriet Dan ... didn't really send me, you know. ... He doesn't know I'm here ... that was a convenient excuse.
Anna 1 What for?
Harriet (*laughing*) I don't know ... (*Bitterly*) There was absolutely no need for me to come here at all—ever. I could have gone to Johannesburg for six months let alone two and the children would just have said, "Oh, have you been away? Was it nice?" Prue is very scrupulous about sending cards and presents for my birthday and Christmas ... Dan doesn't bother of course ... He says he's happy to receive presents from me on the strict understanding that he never reciprocates. He says it is more blessed for me to give than to receive.
Anna 1 He would!

Pause

Harriet How long have you got the lease on this flat?
Anna 1 Mmm? Oh ... Two years.
Harriet Are you settled in your job then?
Anna 1 I suppose so. (*With a smile*) My head of department retires in three years' time ... I'd like her job—I think! It's a pretty good school. Pleasant staff. Nice girls ... OK on the whole. I enjoy my work ... (*Briskly*) It's a thankless job at times of course ... You wonder if you're any use to anyone. (*She stops rather bleakly*)
Harriet I can imagine you being a very good teacher.
Anna 1 (*reflectively*) Yes. Thank you.
Harriet What will you do with the flat if Prue does go abroad?
Anna 1 What?
Harriet If Prue decides to work abroad——

There is an awkward silence

Anna 1 (*cautiously*) She hasn't mentioned that ...
Harriet (*with an undefined hint of malice*) Oh. I'm probably wrong. But she always intended to practise abroad somewhere. When she's finished at the hospital. I can't really see Prue settling in a quiet little group practice can you?
Anna 1 No.
Harriet She always called her father's practice Alcoholics and Geriatrics

Unlimited. She'd never vegetate in the Home Counties. Too much energy.

Anna 1 She's never talked much about her plans ... I suppose I'd have to let her room while she was away ... if she went away.

Harriet Prue's always been a law unto herself. It's not wise to rely on her ... I was a very bad mother. I wasn't really interested in them you see. So I fussed round them both all the time to make up for it. Not a very good idea! I was too much wrapped up in Richard—their father ... my husband. (*With a smile*) But you had children as a matter of course in those days. Richard died seven years ago.

Anna 1 I'm sorry.

Harriet Yes. (*She sighs and crosses and stands looking down at Dan's belongings. Thoughtfully*) Lily's son—that's the friend I was staying with—her son Stephen—lived at home till he was thirty-one. I was always horrified. Your children are supposed to go. Leave the nest. That's what they're for isn't it? Lily—spoiled Stephen ... Then he suddenly got married to an Italian girl and went to live in Florence. Without a backward look. Lily was shattered ... I was looking forward to Prue and Dan being eighteen and striking out on their own. I just felt an enormous sense of—release ... when they went. (*She laughs a little*) Then Richard struck out on his own ... I must be going.

Anna 1 I expect we'll see you again before you go—and when you get back too, I hope!

Harriet (*smiling*) Polite Anna! Goodbye then ... Tell Prue I'll see her when I get back.

Anna 1 Goodbye. *Bon voyage!*

They shake hands. Anna begins to pick up Dan's things. Harriet stops her, collecting them herself

Harriet (*with a smile*) No. I must cultivate self-reliance!

They smile at one another and Anna holds the door for Harriet

Harriet goes out

Anna 1 sees her out then slowly comes back to the middle of the room

Anna 1 "The hall door shuts again and all the noise is gone." Keats ... (*She looks around*) And all the people ... (*She crosses to the window and stands in profile looking out*)

Anna 2 enters, stands opposite Anna 1

The Lights fade with a glowing evening light spilling in through the window. The two women are silhouetted against the livid light

Anna 2 (*softly*) Dusk. Children hurrying home from school. The endless sound of traffic in the distance. The lights going on here and there ... in attics and kitchens. The frost beginning to grip ... still air ... the man next door working feverishly in his garden, desperate to finish pulling up the dead plants before the light fades ... his breath like smoke ...

The incinerator spilling over with spent leaves and flowers. Cold and dark settling on the busy world outside ... outside an empty room.

Anna 1 Breathe on the window pane and write ... "Anna" ... and watch it fade ...

She reaches out and takes Anna 2's hand. They stand clasped hands etched against the window

Prue comes in and switches on the light. The shadows are abruptly dispelled

The two Annas stand separate at the window. Prue is clearly exhausted. She comes in and drops, coat still on, into the chair and closes her eyes

You're very late. I was beginning to get worried.

Prue opens her eyes and focuses blearily on the window

Prue Anna! Good God. (*Yawning*) You haven't waited up for me have you?

Anna 1 I had some work to do.

Prue Oh. (*She closes her eyes*)

Anna 1 Don't go to sleep there, Prue. Get yourself to bed. Would you like some cocoa?

Prue How very fifth form at St Claire's. Have we got any cocoa?

Anna 1 Yes. I think so.

Prue (*drowsily*) I don't think I want any ... it'd only wake me up ... cocoa, firelight and true confessions ... Turn that light off would you? It's hurting my eyes ... In a minute I will summon up the necessary energy to get up and walk to my bedroom.

Anna 1 switches off the overhead light. And switches on the reading lamp by her desk

Just keep hoping, Anna, that when and if you have any kids you don't have to trust them to some poor sod of a junior doctor doing a hundred hour week ... Some of us go mad, you know, and rush screaming into the Thames. What time is it?

Anna 1 Quarter to twelve.

Prue Is that all? Then it must be the day I'm confused about ... or the month ... or the year! (*She throws her head back and closes her eyes and stretches her legs out in front of her*)

Anna 1 crosses over and stands behind her chair. She lightly strokes Prue's cheek with the back of her hand

Anna 1 Poor Prue!

Prue flinches away and sits up abruptly. Anna 1 is surprised

Sorry!

Prue It's all right. I loathe having my face touched.

Anna 1 I'm sorry.

She stands irresolutely beside the chair. Anna 2 comes from the window and stands at the other side of the chair

Your mother left just after you did this morning. She said she'd see you when she got back.

Prue Yes. I expect she will. She'll bring me some litle piece of ethnic tat back with her—to show she's with me really.

Anna 1 You seem to hate her.

Prue No. I don't hate anybody ... She's a bloodsucker. Leeched on to my father for years then when he died she was left without another host to feed on.

Anna 2 (*quietly*) Is that what you think of me?

Anna 1 She told me about your father ... She seemed to love him.

Prue Oh I daresay she did, if love is what she thinks it is.

Prue is almost lightheaded with tiredness and her remarks are dropped casually with no apparent thought, in contrast with Anna who is consumed with a quiet intensity

Anna 1 What do you think love is?

Prue (*cheerfully*) Haven't a clue! Something you treat yourself to when you're feeling flush ... Smoked salmon instead of sardines on toast once in a while and blow the expense.

Anna 1 You sound like Dan.

Prue Aah, you see the same blood pumps through our veins. (*Grinning*) What Mummy has left us that is.

Anna 1 I don't like you talking that way. It's not like you!

Prue No? I am very tired. This is the real me. Not the good little girl with the white ankle socks and the Clarks sandals trotted out for public inspection.

Anna 1 No.

Prue (*wearily*) Anna, I am so tired I am babbling. I've been on duty for thirteen hours. When I can get my legs co-ordinated I'm going to bed.

Anna 1 Do you want me to wake you when I get up?

Prue No thanks.

Anna 1 Prue, are you going to work abroad?

Prue (*looking at her sharply*) Like tomorrow you mean?

Anna 1 No! When you've finished here.

Prue Mummy's been talking to you! "Vengeance is mine. I will repay" ... Probably. I always intended to. (*Her tone is very dismissive. This is not Anna's business as far as she is concerned*)

Anna 1 You never mentioned it— —

Prue Well. I vary a bit. It's not an immediate decision. "Sufficient unto the day" ... She always took it as a criticism of Dad when I said I couldn't work here. (*She gets up*) Perhaps I just want to put at least two continents between me, my mummy and my baby brother.

Anna 2 (*urgently*) What about me? Don't I matter? Haven't you thought of me? Haven't I crossed your mind? I've got to mean something to you even if I'm only a nuisance to be brushed aside. You must take the trouble to brush me aside— —

Anna 1 When will you go?

Prue It won't be for ages. I'll give you plenty of warning. Anyway you might go first.

Anna 1 I doubt it.

Anna 2 No I can't. I won't. I have come here. There's nowhere else for me to go.

Anna 1 I'd quite like it here on my own. It would be peaceful.

Prue Sister Anna!

> "I have desired to go
> Where springs not fail
> To fields where flies no sharp and sided hail
> And a few lilies blow."

Load of rubbish! Miss Thingy—what was she called? That nun that hopped it over the wall and came to teach us English?

Anna 1 Horobin.

Prue Silly cow she was.

Anna 1 is silent

Cheer up! ... I never pretended otherwise ... I'm not responsible for your fantasies, love. I like my job better than anything else I know. I prefer to do it unencumbered. No emotional luggage ... lost in flight.

Anna 1 You sound as though you despise me.

Prue That's what Simon said. I don't. I just don't ask you to mop up after me ... There's real respect for you! But I'm just passing through if you like ...

Anna 2 And going ... Simon ... all those unendurable demands ... And you—like iced water. Refreshing. Cooling. But no nourishment ...

Anna 1 That's fine by me. I'm not a fool ...

Prue *(coolly)* No. Neither's my mother. I despise her though because she wants love without responsibility ... and because—by a biological accident, I'm her daughter, she's fixed on me. Dan's made up his own rules ... everything without responsibility. I'm not much interested in that either ... "I do not look who went before nor who shall follow me. No! At myself I will begin and end." I might have read English, you know, if I hadn't wanted to do medicine. That would have been a nice useless thing to do wouldn't it? I'll see you in the morning ... I'm drunk with tiredness. *(She grins at Anna 1)* I don't suppose I shall remember any of this in the morning. Good-night.

Anna 1 Good-night.

Prue goes out

Anna 1 takes a few steps after her as if to say something more to her. She stops and stares after Prue. There is nothing to say. Anna 1 with a slight smile moves deliberately forward and sits in the chair Prue has vacated. She watches Anna 2 who moves c looking round the empty room

Anna 2 Anna Rose Wentworth. Spinster. History teacher ... Sunny third-floor flat. Immac. decor. Fine view over the park. Cosy bathroom.

Spacious living-room. Would make delightful study or third bedroom. No children. No pets. No sub-letting. NB. No lift. Would suit Anna nicely.

Music. The Lights slowly fade

CURTAIN

FURNITURE AND PROPERTY LIST

ACT I

On stage: Tea-chest. *In it:* mirror
Radiator under window
Telephone

Off stage: Paper, chalk (**Anna 2**)
Chair. *On it:* jacket with cravat in pocket (**Simon**)
Paper (**Anna 1**)
Embroidery ring (**Anna 2**)
Bloodstained handkerchief (**Prue**)
Bowl of hot water, pillowcase (**Anna 1**)
Tray with 3 mugs of coffee (**Simon**)
3 dirty plates and cutlery (**Prue and Simon**)
Rucksack, bed roll, string bag of books (**Dan**)

During Black-out on page 15 set:
Desk. *On it:* pens, pencils etc., desk lamp
Chair
Sofa
Coffee table

Off stage: Pile exercise books, cup of coffee, cassette radio (practical) with tape of
Debussy piano music playing (**Anna 1**)
Suitcase, 2 carrier bags full of odds and ends including books (**Dan**)

Personal: **Anna 1:** wrist-watch
Harriet: handbag

ACT II

Set: Book behind cushion on sofa

Off stage: Tray with pot of tea, cups, saucers, biscuits, jug of milk, lemon etc.
(**Anna 1**)
Pot of tea (**Prue**)

During Black-out on page 31:
Strike tea-tray and set newspaper
Towel (**Anna 1**)
Top-hat (**Simon**)
Bouquet of flowers (**Anna 2**)
Sponge bag (**Prue**)

Personal: **Anna 1:** wrist-watch
Harriet: handbag

LIGHTING PLOT

Practical fittings required: desk lamp, pendant
Interior. An attic room. The same scene throughout

ACT I

To open:	Black-out	
Cue 1	When ready *Bring up general interior lighting*	(Page 1)
Cue 2	**Simon:** "... you move on." *Pause, then fade to oval of light* C	(Page 4)
Cue 3	**Anna 1:** "... No. No. No." *Return to previous lighting*	(Page 6)
Cue 4	**Simon** sets coffee down *Fade lights*	(Page 9)
Cue 5	When ready *Warm lighting over* **Anna 1, Simon** and **Prue**	(Page 9)
Cue 6	**Simon** exits; **Anna 1** stands alone in middle of room *Change lights to cold white; throw shadow effect on floor—* *arched cell window*	(Page 12)
Cue 7	**Anna 2** enters *Backlight her*	(Page 12)
Cue 8	**Anna 2** exits; **Anna 1** moves into her place *Return to previous lighting*	(Page 13)
Cue 9	**Dan** smiles and sits quite still *Fade lights*	(Page 15)
Cue 10	When ready *Bring up general interior lighting*	(Page 15)
Cue 11	**Anna 1** switches on desk lamp *Snap on desk lamp*	(Page 15)
Cue 12	**Anna 1:** "She's crying." *Pause, then slowly fade lights*	(Page 20)

ACT II

To open:	General interior lighting; desk lamp on	
Cue 13	**Anna 1** buries her face in her arms on her lap *Fade to pool of light near desk*	(Page 23)
Cue 14	**Anna 2:** "... the hands reaching——" *Pause, then return to previous lighting*	(Page 24)
Cue 15	**Dan:** "... when we go?" *Fade to spot on Anna 1*	(Page 30)
Cue 16	**Prue, Simon, Dan** and **Harriet** move to sides of set *Backlight figures*	(Page 30)
Cue 17	**Anna 2:** '... quite—quite silent." *Flash lights eerily across stage*	(Page 31)

EFFECTS PLOT

ACT I

ACT II

Printed in Great Britain
by Butler & Tanner Ltd, Frome and London

Lightning Source UK Ltd.
Milton Keynes UK
UKOW06f0108150116

266403UK00013B/109/P